WORK

Brandon Brown

a t e l o s

43

ISBN: 978-1-891190-43-8

First edition, first printing

Thank you very much Derek Fenner, Lyn Hejinian, and Travis Ortiz.

This book is given with gratitude and love to my friends.

 A t e l o s

A Project of Hip's Road
Editors: Lyn Hejinian & Travis Ortiz
Text and Cover Design and Typesetting: Derek Fenner
Cover Image:

The Grass so little has to do –
A Sphere of simple Green –
With only Butterflies to brood
And Bees to entertain –
And stir all day to pretty Tunes
The Breezes fetch along –
And hold the Sunshine in its lap
And bow to everything –

And thread the Dews, all night, like Pearls –
And make itself so fine
A Duchess were too common
For such a noticing –

And even when it dies – to pass
In Odors so divine –
Like Lowly spices, lain to sleep –
Or Spikenards, perishing –

And then, in Sovereign Barns to dwell –
And dream the Days away,
The Grass so little has to do
I wish I were a Hay –

                              Emily Dickinson

"Someone born lucky gets to fuck.
Someone born unlucky goes to work."

                              Bernart de Ventedorn

WORK

at 4:29 p.m. I hear
a little ringing sound
elevator doors part
and I walk out of the
Golden Bear building
at 1995 University Avenue
in Berkeley California,
past the H&R Block sign
that reads OWN YOUR
TOMORROW, flash peace
sign at the guard whose
presence is surprisingly
calming for a kind-of cop.
For the last few weeks
he has been reading the
novels of Toni Morrison,
bored and taskless behind
guard desk. Sometimes I
consider asking him what
he thought of the last
paragraph of *Song of Solomon,*
to me a *Mona Lisa* of prose,
only better than the *Mona
Lisa,* but check myself with
the soft chastisement of
ACAB. Yes even kind
of cops. I saw him once
in civ clothes on a skate
board, the navy starch
of his kind-of-cop costume
conceals pretty good neck
tattoos. I go out glass doors
and it is already dark,

nadir for daylight in
the year and wasn't it
just yesterday I was
arrayed in sun on
the rocks of the Yuba
nourishing what's reptile
inside me, torching fragrant
herb to make the water
softer. Cool dusk. I can
still see the traces of
ancient vomit on side
walk. I admire for a
moment its tenacity
passing by. Like those
attacked by acne as
teens can wear the
souvenirs for a long
time, this one puke
insists on itself, its
meaning the long
afterlife of proteins
remitted to the earth
as barf. Before I went
to work every day in
Berkeley California I
thought it was a bit
enchanted, a place
where an endowed
lectureship in radical
geography meets blazed
demonstration of never-
concluded summer of
love but now I know
it is cursed, inhospitable
to anyone not borne aloft

on the bad effervesce
of cash I guess like
every place in the world.
When your face is wet
with tears in Berkeley some
times you wipe your face
with a McDonald's bag,
you walk by what no
one could possibly tolerate
and call that life in the city,
or, you know, Berkeley.
Waiting to cross broad
avenue, I see a robot
squat to pavement, its
brand informing passers-
by it is the semi-living
property of "Sushinista"
an inferior fusion sushi
burrito enterprise nearby.
As always I daydream of
delivering Nike kick to
its metallic esophagus
breaking its thyroid
cartilage and liberating
its spirit for the heaven
of food delivery robots.
They have these
little eyes, you know?
That look up imploring
glance against such
violence and yet it would
be so satisfying. The other
day Lyn said "I saw a
dead robot" and I thought
that's the first time I've

heard anyone say that
but it will not be the last.
Do you think these little
fuckers have memories?
I asked Maged the other
day about that since he
works robot-adjacent:
will they remember us?
Not just the ephemeral
desire which seizes
us now and then
for weak fucked up
sushi burritos, but
our daydreams and
desires, our wanting
to smash in metal
sides with our feet.
Will they be coming
to our homes with
their own Nikes, ready
for revenge? For now
it is a mellow antebellum
before they become our
masters. Maged just
laughed, which first
amused and then felt
ominous. I do not kick
over the "Sushinista"
robot. At the cross
walk, the lights turn,
little white humanoid
shape, legs askance,
offers permission to
advance. So I walk
alongside robot, its

dinky wheels treading
road, two pedestrians
trying to stay alive.
All the cars are waiting
to turn and I see the
bloodthirsty look on
their drivers' faces.
They too want to smash
the little machine into
asphalt, a flat pond
of metal guts, its bones
would stud the ground
ever after, its blood
and vital juices
staining the sidewalk.
A little like that
vomit. Some of the
cars probably want
to do the same with
me, walking too slowly
in the daydream of my
poem. I walk down
Milvia Street, past ugly
new condos, past ACE
hardware store blazed
alight with the colors
of Christmas, you know
the ones, and guy with
his dog selling *Street
Spirit* for one dollar.
But I have the *Street Spirit*
and I don't have a dollar
in my pocket so
I wish guy and dog
a good day, to which

they reply Merry Christmas
to which I have no
answer. I cross Addison
and at Center I cross
the street and continue
down to the corner of
Allston. I make this
walk down Milvia
every day and I never
make the walk without
remembering the day
several hundred white
supremacists, neo-nazis,
fascists, emissaries from
the ugly pond peoples
of furthest Kekistan,
and unaffiliated right
wing fuckfaces gathered
in MLK park. Right
here at Center we
saw two teenagers
wearing full suits
of armor march past,
headlong into squall of
black bloc. They came
back two minutes later,
gassed in the eyes
and I walked into
the street in front of
them, seized with
sudden rage and
Schadenfreude
suggesting that they
complement their
burning eyes by

fucking killing
themselves when
they got back to mom's
house. It was a
Saturday. I was very
clearly not at work.
Later, a smaller squad
of white supremacists,
neo-Nazis, fascists,
emissaries from the
ugly pond peoples
of furthest Kekistan
and unaffiliated alt-
right fuckfaces marched
down Shattuck sieg-heiling.
By then, we were at home,
watching the Warriors
beat the Rockets. On
the following Monday
I ran into J in the
lobby of the Y
and asked him how
his ankle was feeling
after one of the fascists
in the park exercised
their precious pre-
rogative to free
speech in the form
of a hurled rock
which landed in a
tender place. He
was ok, could do
some squats. I signed
up for a personal
training session and told

my person I needed
to exercise the muscles
necessary for hand to
hand combat. But this
evening there are
no visible white
supremacists, neo-Nazis,
fascists, emissaries from
the ugly pond peoples
of furthest Kekistan
or unaffiliated alt-right
fuckfaces. I pass
the entrance to the
YMCA Hotel, the spot
where you suddenly
smell a rush of chlorine,
pure pool, toxic and nasty
and inviting to those
of us who love to be
in water no matter
how much it reeks.
I like some people
who do not want
to be always in the
water but there will
be a permanent wedge
between us, especially
in the summer which
it is decidedly not
yet. I turn corner
and walk into the Y,
use card to access
turnstile, which beeps
and clicks. Someone
says have a good

work out. I grab
wan white towel
from stacked rolls
on desk and say
thank you you too.
I go into locker
room which smells
like sweat, spray
deodorant, calcified
BO, find a locker,
stash tote I guess
I stole from Kathleen
and Peter when
they left it at our
house and I forgot
and keep forgetting
to return it. It's a fucked
up and wonderful bag.
Mickey and Minnie Mouse
hold hands next to that
big Looney Tunes bird,
Porky Pig, Snoopy in
his JOE COOL shirt,
Garfield with the big
smile of a cat who
has just devoured
a large lasagna. The text
reads MERCY VILLAGE
and I cannot imagine
what such a village
would be to accommodate
this contrafactual crew
of fictional characters.
It's a humiliating accessory.
I try to remember

to wear it with
the artwork and text
turned toward armpit
to conceal my shame
and yet it is such a
spacious sack, so sturdy,
I suppose I will need
to return it or maybe
not until this book
comes out if they read it
hi Kathleen hi Peter
I take off shoes, all my
clothes, dangle goggles
off one finger, draw
on Speedo and grope
towards showers, not
seeing much without
glasses, smudge of
bodies. One of the rituals
which precedes swimming
in the pool is to wet
the body with shower
before wetting it with
pool. Hair sinks under
weight to head, soggy
hamstrings under butt.
I carefully walk along
the side of pool to edge,
nod at bored lifeguard
suffering the indignity
of working, their task
not improved by poolside
office. Slide into pool,
shiver. I submerge
to overcome initial

bracing then stand,
water cooling on
tips of my nipples,
adjust my goggles,
squat, push off wall
with both feet. The
pool, as I was just
telling Stephanie in
my head, is a para-
doxical geometry,
rectangular and five
feet deep, but somehow
permitting infinity of
motion, expansion and
dilation of the body's
threads, which are also
watery. Then I start
to count. I do sixteen
strokes of freestyle then
arc up to inhale to left,
then ten, then eight, then
six, then settle into rhythm,
breathing every four
strokes focused on keeping
my trunk steady and
rocking slightly side to
side as I move through
meters, concentrating
to kick in rhythm with
the movements of my
shoulders and arms.
I do ten laps, rest,
stretch, drink water,
water not poisoned by
the chlorine and other

toxic chemicals which
make the pool clean,
but just regular water,
poisoned with, oh god,
whatever, rest a few
more seconds, then do
another ten laps, then
stretch and rest again
and then another ten,
then stretch and rest
again, and then breast
stroke down and back,
backstroke down and
float back, concluding
my swim. I focus on
huge sign on facing
wall, cheap word cloud
writ large, made to
motivate those swimming
on their backs in the pool
or panting for breath at
pool's edge looking up,
little words, fat with
meaning but dumb in
context: Happy. Feel
Better. Breathe. Motivating
imperatives I guess, and
I'm glad they do not say
Be Stressed. Give Up. Go
Die. Feel Dread. Because
I do not feel dread. I'm
in the pool, almost always
a bulwark against most
bad feeling. Swimming
laps is flourishing and

lifting up your neighbor
in the Spinozan sense,
our body's powers
in service to each other,
dancing core to core,
parting sheets of water
in pool. For much
of my swim I can see
bottom of pool,
clumpy white paint
flaking off, a habit
I acquired swimming
winters in Liberty,
MO under the tutelage
of Coach Dave
"Weed" Wedemyer.
I was a slow swimmer
relative to the studs
of the winter swim
league. Driving back to
Kearney from Liberty
we would listen to
the radio DJ count
down the day's top
ten and that's how
we could tell the time.
Our practice pool was
in a retirement home
and was also used by
the Boy Scouts, who
were rumored to display
wild incontinence, pissing
and shitting right there
in the water and indeed
one season you could see

through goggle's plastic,
in the pool's corner
a hazy turd, petrified
by chlorine like a
sausage in its casing.
I imagined it flavoring
our water and I hated
that. I get out of the water
and consider the hot tub
full of bodies I still
can't see. It's too crowded
so settle for steam room.
First drop Speedo in
old loud swimsuit dryer,
then fold dryish Speedo,
set them near bench
and go into steam room
with the crappy white
towel of the Y.
Sweat or whatever it
is starts to dot my torso
and neck, moisture under
balls and butt and onto
towel, back of knees.
I zone out in the moisture
and heat, watching my
upper arm turn salmon,
then radish. Every time
a naked guy comes
into the room a quick
inhale of regular cold
gymnasium air lessens
the heat and thickness of
the steam. And thus I come
to hate everyone who

enters the room. When
it is really so hot that
I can't stand it I rise
from tile, head woozy
for a second as the air
is actually hotter as you
rise, go into shower and
turn water on, cold
at first, then rising to meet
temperature of my body,
squirt soap onto my hand
and use it as a sponge
to clean my armpits, cock
and balls and butt and
rinse everything and finger
shampoo into my hair,
tangled and brittle from
its time in chlorine, and
then turn off shower
and dry off with towel
I brought from home,
compared to the one
from the Y, a Porsche.
Then stand under hair
dryer mounted on wall
and dry hair for thirty
seconds, then pause by
scale to dry feet as I am
nervous to slip on
dewy gym floor,
likewise do not want
to leave my own water
where somebody else
will slip and fall
and die on the floor

of the gym and their
death will be on my
hands. I step on the
scale, look at the number,
246, close my eyes
in soft shame. Then walk
over to locker, unhinge
brass lock, put on
boxers, deodorant, comb
hair back, slick it with
pomade, drape shirt
across my torso and
button from the top
down, tuck into chinos,
pull socks onto feet
and tie shoes, then zip
gym bag and pivot
towards door when
I notice my gym crush
standing next to me,
combing long auburn
hair straight before work
out. I know you are not
supposed to have a gym
crush. I hope you will
trust that I am a low-key
crusher in this regard
have of course never
talked to them or even
made eye contact or
really even looked at
them and yet their beauty
is like in one of those
stupid fables of Welsh
mythology, where some

unlucky aristocrat rides
horse into a field and
encounters the most
beautiful person in
the world, prompting
a series of trials and
labors effected by love
for them, which are not
quite "work" but typically
do suck. I toss the Y
towel into bin and
walk out of the gym
where it is already dark
as midnight on a moon-
less night, walk up Allston
to Shattuck by scattered
squads of Berkeley High
students, little assholes.
I trudge behind one
group of three. One
of them tells the other
two that they are so
tired because someone
came over at four a.m.
for a "dick appointment"
the friends take this in
stride. And I do too.
And I too used to be
covered in the damn dew.
At Shattuck I shuffle
down stairs to the station
and tap Clipper card.
A dude hurdles turnstile
next to me, delicious
extinguished blunt in

mouth. I hope my body
has helped shield him
from the BART police.
I walk the length of
platform to the rear of
train. Richmond in 5
and 13. From the platform
I can see into the bowels
of the track where
there is a sweater, a
syringe, and empty
plastic bottle of Taaka
vodka, the size I used
to buy nightly after
a shift at the café bar
I worked at, stirring
with ginger ale to court
sleep over ice. We called
them "little guys" to
contrast its relative
moderation compared
to its older brother,
a "big guy," reserved
for those nights when
you wanted to properly
drink into stupor
I'd usually settle for a
little guy, inhaling Parliament
smoke and the aromas of
my job at the café bar,
espresso and IPA.
I take big book out of bag,
it's *Bullshit Jobs* by
David Graeber and hold
in hand as first sound

then light of train pulls in
and I pack in among tired
workers going home.
Graeber's book evolves
from the insight that
"huge swaths of people,
in Europe and North
America in particular,
spend their entire working
lives performing tasks
they secretly believe
do not really need to be
performed." I almost
never read books about
work, just as I will
never watch *The Office,*
it is always and ever
too soon for that. But
I thought I might
learn something about
myself from *Bullshit Jobs,*
I mean not myself but
my predicament. Graeber
by the way does not
mean "shitty jobs" by
"bullshit jobs" in fact
what he calls shitty jobs,
the ones held by bus
drivers and gardeners
and baristas and cooks,
are, for him, instances
of meaningful work that
instill pride in workers,
their capacity to serve
and drive around and

manicure property
and serve lattes and
prepare food. For Graeber,
it's those who work
in bureaucracies, as I do,
who truly pursue the
bullshit jobs. In the chapter
I'm reading he proposes
a thought experiment:
"imagine if a certain class
of people were to simply
vanish" by which he
means nurses, garbage
collectors, grocery store
clerks, and teachers, the
world as we know
it would cease to be.
But if hedge fund
managers, marketing
gurus, lobbyists, bankers,
also all of what we call
"administrative professionals,"
if these people were to
disappear, who would
fucking care. His
example is the pitiful
university staff whose
job one day became
apologizing to Professor
David Graeber when
someone didn't come
to fix his office book
shelf quickly enough.
Graeber not only declines
to accept this apology,

he makes the sorry staff
a member an example
of the world's violent
meaningless in *Bullshit Jobs.*
The passage makes me
angry and I facial my
rage for the tired commuters
going home from their
jobs to El Cerrito, El
Cerrito del Norte, or
Richmond, or indeed
beyond Richmond. I mean
Graeber isn't wrong,
these and all jobs are
of course bullshit. But
I find the idea that all
these jobs are bullshit
and yet his job, professor
of anthropology at a
university, somehow trans-
cends these other kinds
of jobs, suspect to say
the least. I close the book
and tuck into jacket
pocket as the train declines
into El Cerrito, doors
part with noise like a metal
show and I file down the
stairs one at a time in dense
mob, then tap Clipper card
on the turnstile. And
walk out of the El Cerrito
Plaza BART Station, jay
walk across the road
and check behind my

shoulder to look at times
for the next trains arriving,
a tic I don't understand
as I am not going to work,
I am no longer waiting
for a train and yet I never
fail to look. Walk across
the parking lot swerving
in between gaps in parked
cars and parking spot
seekers, then walk down
a small grassy decline onto
sidewalk at Fairmount
and cross the street.
I walk down Fairmount
cross Liberty, like
the town in Missouri
next to the one I grew
up in, the ancestral
home of Coach Dave
"Weed" Wedemyer.
I put my headphones in
and play "This Is The Way
We Ball" by Lil Flip
a song I listened to
frenzied for a year
and promptly forgot
the existence of until now.
It sounds great, Flip's
melodic delivery unearthing
such surprising lines as
"I make rainbows when
the sun reflects off my
tooth." Then pivot and put
on Joni Mitchell's *Blue,*

an album I will never
be exhausted by although
I smile thinking that Alli
would disapprove, since
she has a theory that
there are only very
particular times and
places when and where
one should properly risk
the emotional Vesuvius
Blue is, and a walk home
from the train on the
longest night of the year
is probably not one of
them. Ahead big Albany
Hill, its foliage pointillist
in darkness. It is the hill
for which El Cerrito is
named. I love to look
at it but will never climb
again, especially on a night
this dark. The one morning
I did I saw a creepy cat
crouched under a tree.
I was wearing narrow
leather dress shoes
after being coerced
into breakfast with
colleague from work,
invitations I typically try
to deflect but which
occasionally I feel compelled
to sustain, to maintain
appearance of an obsequious
servant who can get along

well with whoever, whenever.
The cat stared me down and
followed me with its
eyes as I walked by. Even
fifteen, twenty feet, twenty
five feet, down the trail
I looked back and it was
still staring at me. Brrr.
That day I walked from
Albany Hill on this path
to BART, it was the day
I first heard "Malibu"
by Miley Cyrus and
then got a text from
Alli that said someone
had been murdered
in Charlottesville and
I stopped right here,
on Liberty Street to read
the news and my guts
went into my neck
and I considered throwing
up right there on Fairmount
Street, barf somebody
would have to clean up
someday I guess, but
decided to keep walking
to the train, texting Alli
what in the fuck and
that was more or less
the last time I listened
to "Malibu." I walk by
the great stores of the El
Cerrito Plaza's north side:
T-Mobile, Tapioca Tea Bar,

vintage donut shop in white
and red like a barber
shop of sugar and fat,
Starbucks. After Liberty
is Kearney, spelled exactly
like my hometown and
I wonder if it is pronounced
same and I remember my
shame moving to San Francisco
and finding people here
pronounce "Kearny" like
"Cur-knee" not "Car-knee"
which I realized is the
effect of a drawl common
to honkies in my childhood
region I mean they called
a bear a "bar." Strange
to live in a place now
where every day I cross
first Liberty then Kearney
and later Kearney and
then Liberty, two words
which signify adolescence
to me, two remote towns
studding rural highway,
descending into white
nightmare the further
distance from the city.
If Liberty was Kansas
City's lesser moon
Kearney was practically
its Neptune. My brother
just posted this beautiful
thing on Facebook,
listening to the Royals

radio announcer who has
called games since we
were both kids: "It's
beyond my ability to
describe how or why
listening to Denny
Matthews tell me about
the upcoming 'Whit
Merrifield Oven Glove'
promotion in great
detail and as only he
can is such a great,
simple pleasure. Then
that he reminds me
of Denny in the 1980's
imploring us to enjoy
some Guy's nuts and
potato chips. Then
I can and do close
my eyes and literally
smell the smell of
driving past the Guy's
factory in Liberty, MO.
Which then makes me
think of the William
Jewell frat boys who
would lay out on lawn
chairs on their frat house
roofs, which just seemed
unbelievably dangerous
and cool and hard for a
six year old to even
fathom the logistics of,
and who you would
pass on the way past

the Guy's potato chip
factory." Past Kearney
is the Pic n'Pac liquor
store where I cross
through the parking lot
past person in car
unwilling to wait to
get home for big
cold first drink of
beer. Pause at San
Pablo for the light to
change and on the
sidewalk there is a
plaque which reads
El Cerrito's First Mayor,
grayscale portrait
white man's face in
a dark suit and white
shirt. "El Cerrito
became a city on August
23, 1917. Businessman
Phillip Lee helped
lead the incorporation
effort and raised funds
for essential services,
including fire and police
protection. Lee was
elected to the City
Council multiple times
and served as mayor
from 1918-24 and 1926-28.
His home and business
were just east of here."
I cross San Pablo and
look north to the big

sign for Nation's Burgers
and on the other side
of the avenue another
plaque: RUST. Tintype
of old-west commercial
strip, Rust Hardware,
the caption reads "In
1915, this handsome
building stood at 10057
San Pablo Avenue. This
area of El Cerrito
was named for early
resident and blacksmith
Wilhelm (aka William) Rust.
The Rust post office was
located near here and
the highest point in
El Cerrito, north of
Arlington Park, was
named William Rust
Summit in 1988."
Prior to being called
"Rust" the land now
called El Cerrito was
part of the Rancho
San Pablo, a 17,939
acre land grant owned
by Francisco Maria Castro,
a rich colonial soldier
in the De Anza expedition
for whom many streets
and caves and hills and
bluffs and towns and parks
are named including
the Castro district in

San Francisco. Before
Francisco Maria Castro
was "awarded" the land
known as Rancho San
Pablo, the land was
inhabited for many
centuries by the Ohlone
people. I read a book
about the Ohlone people
called *The Ohlone Way.*
Maybe you have read
it too. It is written by
Malcom Margolin,
a white person of
European ancestry
with a fair amount
of apologies but I
dunno it felt worth-
while anyway to
read especially if you
live near or in El Cerrito.
If Malcom Margolin
had had the opportunity
to write the text for
a sidewalk plaque
commemorating
the Ohlone people
who lived for centuries
in the land now known
as "El Cerrito" he
might write: "women
scan the meadow—
brome grasses are ripe
and ready to be collected--
they remove small scoops

from their larger baskets
and wade into the tall
grass among flowers,
sweeping through the
seed, loosening the
nutrient-rich seeds
into her basket."
There are a couple
more of these plaques
in El Cerrito, one for
the Cerrito Creek
mildly trailing off to
the side of the mall,
wimpy rivulet. And
there's another one
that informs pedestrians
that El Cerrito is home
to some of the most
important 20th century
rock n'roll bands, that is,
Creedence Clearwater Revival
and Green Day. Across San
Pablo I walk by the bus
stop where a woman splayed
across both seats is talking,
impassioned, I hear her say
"I can't believe I was ever
sucking on a female breast
to get milk." I cut through
the parking lot of Ace
Hardware and at the
crosswalk on Carlson
pause on haunches,
cars hard charging by.
It has not always been

such an armistice between
me and these cars. Like
a spiritual Libra I demand
my right to the city be
recognized and affirmed
but saw that death barreled
forth in that path and I
want to live so now I wait
on my most agreeable
behavior, wave, flash
fingers, hurry to cross.
Sometimes when I am
walking I sing along
out loud to whatever is
playing in my headphones,
conscious usually too late
that it's begun, and I usually
just finish my performance,
as I do now, crossing Carlson,
having swapped Scorpio
singers, Joni for Frank
Ocean, and Frank sings
there's a bull and a mata-
dor dueling in the sky
not dueling but dueting
with Frank. I walk
down San Diego Street
past Yosemite and Santa
Clara, street names that
will prove to you that
you are in California if
you are not sure, and then
take a left on Belmont
which I guess means
"pretty hill," nodding

again to the El Cerrito
up above in shadow
and walk halfway down
the block to our little
yellow bungalow on
the right where we pay
two thousand two hundred
dollars in rent every
month to a landlord we
have never met in order
to live. I go in, unload
my keys and wallet
and Timex and put all
on little wood table built
by Alli's uncle Gary,
the sole smoker in
her family and a person
who I have therefore
leaned on more than
once to bum avuncularly
from. I pick up the mail
on the floor. Safeway
is having a sale on
charcoal but who would
be in the market for
charcoal when it is
winter and dark by
five. Shoppers with
long memories and
foresight I guess, maybe
preppers. Someone wants
to do something to my
student loan. The water
bill has arrived. Drape
blue jacket on the back

of a chair, then pause
to take a look at the
artworks in our living
room. There is a painting
on my left by Matthew
Arnone, a head and back
turned away from the
viewer, chaotic miasma
above the head to the
right of the windows,
a print by Lindsey White,
the image that was on
Alli's first book and which
I tried to buy as a present
but Lindsey insisted it
should be a gift. I in-
sisted in turn it should
be a true trade so on that
note, hi Lindsey, I'm
serious, if there's anything
I can do for you please
let me know. I shelled
out for a beautiful frame
from a pushy guy in a
shop on Shattuck. He
was a real classic frame
store dick, going overboard,
still I let him drain
me, oh well, it looks
great. On the wall
to the right two prints
by Sofía Córdova, a
lily white nuclear
family redacted by
ink, rendering them

as sinister as they
really are and the other,
same size, shows a baby
ungulate, cute and
melancholic, a remnant
of a lost past earth
rendered from the
perspective of a bad
and perilous future
which is often the
setting of Cordova's
work. On the table
below a big granite
boulder which Tamra
Seal found in the desert,
drilled tubular cavity
inside of then stuffed
plastic orange cylinder,
warping the light and
shadows of the room
through interior veins
and arteries of the rock,
slats of brilliant plastic.
It's called *Seeing Through
Things,* and was officially
a trade for a small piece
of writing I did for her
although *Seeing Through
Things* is too generous
a recompense but
Tamra said she consulted
her crystals and they
affirmed for her that
I was the right person
to receive the sculpture

and am I really going
to argue with a sculptor's
crystals no. I go into our
bedroom to change, hang
up shirt, fold pants, stack
on other pairs of folded
pants on closet door,
a habit which annoys
Alli and which I
continually forget
to improve, put on
khaki trousers Alli bought
me and which she calls
"joggers," a word I
have never heard anyone
else say, then a clean
t-shirt. I leave my shoes
on the stairs, the very
step in fact on which
I slipped the night we
moved into our house
in El Cerrito. The Warriors
had just beaten Thunder
in a critical game six.
Klay Thompson dropped
41 on his future teammate
KD, whose nickname is
either "the slim reaper"
or "easy money sniper"
it's up I guess to us.
Buoyed by the win,
the bright new horizon
of having just moved,
a shot or two of mid-
shelf tequila I walked

on air with box of books
when oops. Holding
stiff arm with dislocated
shoulder I said to Alli
I think I broke my arm
I think we need to go
to the hospital. It was
Memorial Day weekend.
The first e-mail I typed
with my functioning left
hand was an e-mail to
boss saying I have
dislocated my shoulder
but I still plan to be at
work on Tuesday but
I did not go to work
on Tuesday. I did go
to work on Wednesday.
I preheat the oven to
three hundred and seventy
five degrees, then wash
dishes from the morning.
Little one cup coffee
maker Alan got me for
my birthday but insisted
was not a "birthday
present," the stupid
SAN DIEGO ZOO
mug from Goodwill
I use every morning,
Alli's mug, my Tupper-
ware, and rinse
French press. I put
olive-colored apron
on, and then the cap

I wear when I cook
now because my hair
is long and I do not
want complaints from
my diners. Tonight, Alli.
The cap is brown and
cream and reads DITCH
WITCH across its front.
I stole it, I guess, from
my sister's husband
Marques over the summer,
we were going to the pool
and I hadn't brought a cap.
"He has so many hats," my
sister said he'll never miss
this one. I didn't know
what a DITCH WITCH
was and actually I still
do not know what a
DITCH WITCH is but
I love it. Cream and brown,
two morphemes independent
rhyming couplet
vaguely occult and
kinky and weirder-sounding
than whatever it really means.
I retrieve spaghetti squash
from chipped ceramic
bowl on credenza where we
keep produce you don't
need to refrigerate like
onions, sweet potatoes,
oranges, blood oranges,
squash. Spaghetti squash
is banana colored blimp

but light for its size.
I pierce canary skin
with sharp knife, and
part in twain, scoop its
seeds out, a cooking
task I don't love,
seeding a squash like
gutting fish, slimy
seeds and earthy odor
which I can never smell
without recalling Robert
Glück's observation
in *Jack the Modernist*
that the inside of Jack's
ass "smelled like a
pumpkin" so I smell
inside of the squash
and think of Bob and
wonder what his method
is for cooking spaghetti
squash and I will ask
him. I line baking sheet
with thin tin foil
and balance squash
on top of slick lining
of olive oil, tuck it
far back in the oven
for greatest encounter
with heat, where it will
bake for one hour. I go
into our bedroom and
fall onto the bed, under
the great woven tapestry
of a Jaguar eating a heart
we bought in Oaxaca.

First I asked the woman
selling it how much it
cost and when she said
two thousand pesos
I thought it was too much.
Alli and I went out into
the plaza by the market,
sat on a bench debating
this purchase. I smoked
a cigarette. I thought
it was too extravagant
and Alli, usually the frugal
one of us, intuited that
my life would never
be as good without
the tapestry of the jaguar
eating a heart and con-
vinced me that I could
part with one hundred
US dollars or there-
abouts and so I went
back in and asked *me
puedes dar la alfombra
de jaguar?* And thanked
its maker and carried
it with us for days
from Oaxaca back
to Mexico City, then
to Oakland where it
hung above my black
leather couch in living
room, pride of the
apartment, a boon to
see for guests of my
court. At our place we

have it above the bed.
Alli said that the red
vaguely fruitish blob
the jaguar places in
its mouth was a strawberry
and indeed similarly
sized and colored shapes
seem to adorn the
background trees but no
a jaguar does not eat
strawberry but will
happily devour fresh
red heart. I try to
read one chapter of
The Brothers Karamazov,
in which Ivan Karamazov
sits in his bedroom,
delirious with stress,
talking to the devil.
I am loving *The Brothers
Karamazov* but I am
suddenly tempted by
the arrival of the sandman,
who tugs my eyelids
down towards cheeks,
dangling the precious
nectar of unplanned
sleep, so delicious, so
wrong, and instead
of softening in the
sandman's mellow
clutch, I take out my
phone and spread it like
the flesh of a cooked
squash. I read the tweets

of Jaylen Brown for
a while, a basketball
player I adore. His
teammates tried to
nickname him "the
poet," which he refused.
"Call me anything but
a poet," he said. Brown
went to Berkeley and I
sometimes joke that I am
going to ask my professor
friends which one of them
ruined poetry for Jaylen
Brown— just kidding
poetry has always
been ruined by, uh,
poets. I look at pictures
of some people's dinner,
pets, bright foliage, selfies,
looming redwoods bending
California light into pale
shape, someone's reading
Yoko Ono's *Grapefruit,*
tween up to neck in water
on a beach, an ad for stupid
restaurant, karaoke, street
porcupine in Slovenia,
Katy Perry in a strange,
and, let's just face it,
bad dress, ads for Toyota
cars, an exquisite pass
by Steve Nash in 1999,
babies, shadow of a star
on the sidewalk, jewelry
for sale, a bunch of trash,

usies, theyies, and one
picture of a hand-dryer
sitting in a toilet. I text
Gina "I love Jaylen Brown"
because there are only
a few people I can text
this thought who will
maybe care, and Gina
will at least understand.
I consider typing
"Jaylen Brown highlights"
into the browser of my
phone but the timer goes
off, the squash is ready.
I take it out of oven
and set its big oblong
blimp shape on
cutting board to cool,
then I heat two table-
spoons of olive oil in
big nonstick pan,
mince four cloves
of garlic, I can feel
my tender fingertips
taking on their aroma,
combine the garlic
and a couple of table-
spoons of bread crumbs
which sizzle in fat
and start to smell
inviting. I wait one
long minute, turn off
heat, then cut ends
of soft squash and
slice in half, then

scoop edible, delicious
flesh from the cavity
of squash, which un-
ravels in goopy guitar
strings. I toss them
with bread crumbs
and garlic and heat
it all together with
a couple more table-
spoons of olive oil.
Alli comes in, shiny
and tired from the
gym. Girlfriend! I say,
wildly misstating what
she is to me. Hi
baby, we both
say and kiss. She
slides into bedroom
to change and I chop
half a cup of
parsley to finish dish.
Spoon squash, crumbs,
and garlic onto white
plates, scatter verdant
herb over and shake
last pinch of salt, fill
up glasses with water
from bottles in fridge
which Alli thinks makes
it taste better, the
temperature I mean.
We remark on the food
as we eat it, that the
combination of squash,
garlic, and salty bread

crumbs is great and
spaghetti squash is so
weird meaning it's a
goddamn miracle,
vegetable with noodle
guts, breathing pasta,
disguised as yellow
football, and tastes
terrific. We talk about
our days, which, even
though mostly what we
both did was sit motionless
at our respective offices,
we do not talk about
that. Alli tells me what
she read on her lunch
break, a new book by
Silvia Federici. I had
coffee with Eric and
say Eric's fine, we talked
about this and that. We
talk about the terrible
things we saw poets
do and say on the
internet, and soon
the squash has left
our plates and become
part of us. We discuss
our respective plans
for the evening. Then
Alli does the dishes
and I spoon the leftover
squash into two glass
containers for tomorrow's
lunch, and clean the

stove with industrial
cleaner which is very
bad to breathe and
touch with the skin
and Alli says don't
forget to clean the
knobs so I don't.
Then wipe stove
dry of grease and
stuck dust. We agree
again that dinner
was good, then offer
temporary farewells.
She goes into the
bedroom and closes
the door to read. I fill
a tall glass with one
big ice cube, a dash
of old fashioned bitters
and a can of La Croix
"pure." Water sizzles
on the cold surface
of the ice as if it were
hot. Then clean
little blue glass pipe
with fingertip and pack
fresh with firm sativa
from Humboldt county
and sprinkle a little
burnished keef on
top, cherries on baby
ice cream cone. Flick
lighter and breathe in
smoke, burn and
cough, the keef sweet

but harsh. Big drink
of my soda which
adds a burp to
the cough. My throat
is tickled and then
it is suave. Take
another contemplative
pull from pipe, then
grab glass and sip,
it is bronze and
sparkly and so good.
I go on Amazon.com
and rent *Marie Antoinette*
which I have twenty
four hours to watch.
Marie Antoinette is a
film by Sofia Coppola
which I rented because
the other night after
a reading Jacq and
Isabel and Kyle all
said *Marie Antoinette*
was great and I believe
them. It costs $2.99
to rent the film. I
agree to terms
and to conditions.
Watching a movie
isn't exactly "working,"
not in the sense that
Alli is "working"
in the bedroom, but
I always remember
Stacy saying that
even when you're

not writing you are
writing, maybe
especially when you
are not writing, so
I recall that and lean
into the ascending
ripples of the weed
and push play and
watch *Marie Antoinette.*
From the credits,
Coppola keys the film's
palette, hot pink,
every range of pink
really, lots of blues,
dull to bright. It sounds
like a film about gender,
and it is, but it is also
about work, which is
only odd in the sense
that Marie Antoinette
doesn't do much
work, and her husband
the king of France,
doesn't do much
of anything at all.
Almost all of their
time is spent lying
on soft silk sheets,
eating massive platters
of roasted quail and
pink and blue and
chocolate desserts,
gossiping, shopping,
riding out to hunt the
stag, gambling, drinking

champagne, talking
relentless and ruthless
shit on each other. Even
the one area of production
which is most prized by
the Queen and King and
the nobility of France, the
production of an heir,
is ignored by Louis.
He won't even try to
fuck Marie, not a good
approach to marriage
with a Scorpio. But
from the film's very
beginning, the service
that Marie and Louis
receive is ceaseless.
Marie Antoinette had
about five hundred
servants, people paid
by the Ministry of the
Royal Household.
The servants tie dainty
laces of Marie's shoes,
they comb her hair,
fold her dress, guard
her bedroom, open
and close the doors,
help her into carriages,
drive the carriages,
they undress her
and dress her, they
hold her dog, they
unpack her trunks
when she travels,

they get the queen
and king ready for
bed and they cover
them with expensive
sheet, and they
pull the curtain
shut above them
as they sleep and
they open it in the
morning, they dress
the Queen, they take
the gloves off the hands
of the Comtesse de Provence
they drape napkins across
their laps and serve food,
of course they make
the food, they bring them
fancy mineral water from
the Ville d'Avray,
better than the swill
from the Seine which
the proles drank to live,
they fuck the King to
give him pleasure,
they spray Marie
with perfume to
increase her sexual
desirability, they do
these things every
day, multiple times,
they dry Marie off
after a bath, they obviously
filled the bath, they
bring in boxes of
shoes from Paris,

they help the King
onto his horse to better
hunt the stag, they
deliver their babies,
they tailor their clothes
and do their hair and
makeup, they announce
the death of the King
and they say long live
the King. They teach
Marie to play the harp-
sichord. They breastfeed
their babies, row their
gondolas, paint her
portrait, they act on
the stage in the play
she presents and stars
in, portraying a simple
peasant wife with a
broom, the irony
hilarious for the King
and the friends of
the King, they art handle
the portrait when one
of the kids dies and has
to be painted out of the
picture. They carry his
little coffin down the
church stairs. They
clean their eggs. They
tell them that the Bastille
prison has fallen, they
die when the palace
is raided, they pack
the bags of nobles as

they flee Versailles,
and tie their robes
before they sneak
off in a secret passage-
way to avoid being
murdered by a mob,
some of them will go
to the scaffold and have
their heads sliced off
by a guillotine on her
account. I get up to pee
about halfway through
and then go into the
bedroom where Alli
is reading and ask her
if she wants to put
down her book and
watch the end of
Marie Antoinette and
Alli just says have they
cut her head off yet.
The film hews pretty
closely to what seem
to be the facts of Marie
Antoinette's life. The
little dog she had to
leave at the French
border along with
her Austrian clothes
was really named
"Mops" I guess, not
that Marie Antoinette
knew what a fucking
mop was but anyway
there are some details

it leaves out in the
interest of time I guess.
And there are obviously
some embellishments
like Marie Antoinette
didn't really drink, but
Dunst's queen is a soft
lush, savoring the sweet
sparkly wine of Alsace
as much as the udder-fresh
milk on her little country
estate. If you know only
two things about Marie
Antoinette, then you
probably know that she
supposedly said, when
one of her attendants
remarked that the poor
people in Paris had no
bread to eat, "let them
eat cake!" and that
she was brought to
the scaffold in the
middle of Paris and
beheaded by the
guillotine. *Marie
Antoinette* depicts the
former, in an understated
scene, showing Dunst
in the bathtub, smiling
with her enormous
mouth and shimmering
molars, *let them eat cake!*
Giggle but then cuts to
a scene of her with her

friends, collectively
pissed at the gossip
being shared in Paris,
"I would never say
that sort of thing,"
the sort of statement
usually made by someone
who definitely would say
that sort of thing. And
then Coppola's major
narrative intervention
is to avoid the execution
scene of Marie Antoinette
entirely. The film's
concluding sequence
shows the queen and
king sitting at their
big banquet table, in
front of what appears
to be a three-layer
vegetable cheesecake.
They look at each
other meaningfully
as the noise outside
the palace increases in
both volume and intensity.
The republicans are coming
and they are armed and
pissed. Marie tenderly
takes Louis's hand, and
then we see that the pastel
cheesecake is gone and they
are left with a comparatively
simple roulade of rare,
expensive white asparagus,

unseasonably appearing
in chilly October. The
next thing we see is
the royal couple led
out of Versailles and
trundled into common
carriage for their trip
to prison. Marie looks
out the window. Louis
smiles. Marie says "I'm
just saying goodbye."
The final scene of
the film is a quiet
shot of one of the
palace's many ball-
rooms. All the chandeliers
and lamps lie on the
ground in shatters.
Someone will have
to come and clean
it up. But that we do
not see. As we do not
see the last days
of Marie Antoinette,
when she is put on
trial by the revolutionary
committee on public
safety and accused
of jerking off the little
dauphin and then
sentenced to death
and dressed in rags
and dragged to
scaffold and brought
up to guillotine where

she stepped on someone's
foot and said I'm so
sorry I didn't mean to
do that and then knelt
and had her head
placed in the guillotine
and the blade dropped
and separated her
head from her body.
When the film is over
I pour bourbon half-
way up the side
of one of the little
crystal glasses Alli's
brother got us for
Christmas, out of six
we have only ruined
four with chips and
cracks, then add a
quarter teaspoon
of bitters I made
to promote active
dreaming and a big
ice cube to make it
chill. The herbs
in it are mugwort,
lavender, lady's
mantle, bay leaf. I go
into our room where
Alli is still reading
and suggest that we
watch NBA highlights
and she agrees, putting
aside her book. The
Nets beat the Rockets

in overtime despite
James Harden dropping
57. Joel Embiid waving
arms in leading the
crowd to chant TRUST
THE PROCESS God
I love Joel Embiid and
would like to get to
know him and be
friends with him in
real life. We skip a
blowout or two,
catch close finish
between Nuggets and
Jazz. The Joker went
off for 40 and 12. Next
I suggest we watch
the day's top plays
Ro Parrish proclaims
top tiiiiiiiiiin to win!
Alli concedes. Ro counts
down today's pantheon—
a disrespectful dunk
puts Mason Plumlee
on a poster, Chris Paul
breaks ankles in Brooklyn,
and then we decide it's
time for bed. Alli
goes to wash her
face and I take one last
stroll through the internet,
flaneurie in a dumpster.
I see a picture of KD
stalking arena hallway,
his silhouette hooded

and carrying a sickle.
"The Slim Reaper."
Cruise past ad for Reese's
dipped pretzels, selfie,
usie, streetlamp illuminating
eerie empty basketball
court, clouds over
mountains in Finland,
Christ how dark is it
there? Charli XCX in
lingerie. Then I go into
the bathroom and brush
my teeth then floss, an
activity I was just telling
Sara I love now when
I do it I feel like I am
taking extremely good
care of myself. Because
I have modest gum
disease, I must scrup-
ulously floss. I use
a pick for my front
teeth with a bronze
rubber-tipped tool
that never fails to
excavate gross white
paste of former food
cornering where floss
is not permitted to
probe. I rinse and
spit the tasty water
of El Cerrito. I rub
face cream across
my cheeks and forehead
and eye cream under

my eyes, bend again
to wipe errant drops
of pee off floor and
toss, flush, then show
Alli my new muscles
before getting into bed
and making a big fuss
about how cold it is,
my nightly stand-up
comedy routine. It's like
fucking Antarctica in here
it's like *I'm sleeping on
top of a damn glacier.*
My buzz and I find
these jokes hilarious.
Alli politely ignores
us both. We kiss.
Then I spray her with
spritz which was birthday
gift from Stephanie, her
eyes closed she is so
beautiful, she sprays
me, we kiss again
and she turns on her
right side and I lean
into Alli and our skin
warms at the same
rate and I reflect
how smart we were
to "switch sides"
after twelve years
of sleeping on respective
sides every night we
slept together, which
was not every night

for 12 years, there
were many years when
we did not sleep together
every night or even
most nights, but we
still always had these
sides, and one night
at Christmas at her
brother's we had to
sleep on the "wrong
sides" for some reason
and it was so wonderful
I could curl against her
back all night without
moving so when we
got back we "switched
sides"and my head sinks
thanks to indica, whiskey,
bay leaf, lady's mantle,
lavender, mugwort.
Five hours later I wake
up and get up in the
dark and try to close
the door as quietly
as I can and decide
between attending to
bladder brimming
with pee or the dream,
and choose the dream.
I was heading down
San Pablo, driving.
I picked up a young
woman who looked
like Tracy, wearing
big fake fur spotted

coat like Lissa used
to wear, and for
some reason we
stopped and she got
out and I drove away,
from the passenger
seat, pressing gas
pedal with my hand.
She almost caught
up running after,
but I finally sped
away and got home.
Alli was there,
hanging out with Julian
and Townes Van
Zandt. I was going
to cook dinner,
but first I needed
to get rid of the
woman's coat and
belongings so she
couldn't find me
and do something
bad to Alli's car.
We had a quick
argument about
whether there was
enough wine. Townes
followed me outside.
He was wearing
one of those down
jackets that make tech
workers look so fucking
stupid and he said...
something...to me

as I left. I walked up
the street and dropped
the coat and was
fishing the woman's
money out of a little
satchel where she
kept it. And then I was
involved in some kind
of a heist. A woman had
seduced me and I had
helped without knowing
what she was doing,
which was "stealing
the Alhambra." Most
of the dream was the
aftermath. I lost my
job and apartment.
Melissa had also been
involved and I asked
her to help me start
over. Shawn Mendes
had been my coworker
and we had both been
fired. We were supposed
to have given a performance
with Hoa Nguyen, who
definitely does not like
me very much, and I
kept asking Shawn if
Hoa was fired too.
I was scared, but real-
ized it was a chance
for Alli and me to move
in together. I was
set to ask her, when

we saw the amazing
sight of a bird taking
her newborn chicks
to the backyard to
eat. They "needed
to eat New York and
New Jersey." I close
the notebook and go
into the bathroom
and pee for what
feels like hours, re-
closing my eyes to
try and get back
into the domain of
sleep, flush toilet
and sneak back
into bed next to Alli,
whose body is a
furnace under blankets
against the cold dark
night of what is now
December twenty
second. The last day
of work before several
days of holidays. It
doesn't take me
long to get back
to sleep. At 6:24 a.m.
my alarm rings and
I panic, roll and pound
it silent, then twist
on my back, eyes
closed, accepting
that I am awake
and that this is

the world I woke
in, Alli breathing
measured, sweet
lump who puts pillow
over head because
when I am up I am
the bringer of noise
and light. I lean over
and kiss the back of
her neck lightly she
doesn't stir. I get up
and pee again, dazed
as yellow stream fills
bowl. The gas trapped
in my guts all night
is liberated and once
or twice therefore
I fart. Then go into
the kitchen and sit
in my boxers and
write down another
dream, somewhat
damaged by my decision
to pee before writing it
down. In the dream
I decided to "shower
at the Y" before work.
There were just two
stalls. In one a deranged
guy had put a bunch
of stuff and said "there
are illegal immigrants
in there." I said "I don't
think that's true" but go
to the other stall which

is occupied so I wait
naked with my towel
but then I'm at work,
at my desk, with Alli
there. I'm writing in
a notebook but I am
certain that it is
"the wrong notebook."
I break a Juul pod
and get the nasty liquid
all over my t-shirt. I tell
Alli that I can get
a replacement pod
but would have to
register online. She
says that sounds like
something you would
do. My boss and coworker
are coming back to where
my desk is. My boss just
nods at Alli, as if they've
never met, which
is odd because they
did meet, "just over
the weekend." That was
it. These are constant
themes in my dreams.
I am always driving a car,
seeing old friends, having
some kind of fight
with Alli in public.
I dream of cinematic
heists, poets, lots of
parties. And most of all
I dream about work.

I close the notebook
then turn the water on
in the shower, which
needs time to warm,
especially on this
darkest day of the year
when it's so cold in
El Cerrito. I walk naked
into the kitchen and fill
electric kettle with water
and turn it on. I take
one Lisinipril, little blue
pill with a bit of water
and check my e-mail
on my phone, nothing
new. Water is hot so
I slide into the shower,
rub face cleanser into
my skin and rinse
it off, then grab green
toothbrush covered in
paste, clean my mouth,
finally soap arms,
underarms, torso,
cock, balls, asshole, rinse.
I've got this song by
Britney Spears called
"Hold It Against Me"
stuck in my head,
a brilliant tune whose
conceit is the simple
inquiry, expressed in
double entendre: if I
want your body now
would you hold it

against me? Dry off
and put clean underwear
on, then rub chalky
Degree Cool Rush
deodorant on underarms,
spread sunblock on my
cheeks and nose, the
back of my neck, my
chin and the front
of my neck tender
skin easily parched
and pruned, even in
so few hours of sun-
light, then comb back
my hair and paste
with dime of pomade,
hum very softly a few
bars of "Hold it
Against Me," go into
kitchen and pour
boiling water over
coffee grounds in the
one-cup coffee maker
Alan got me for my
birthday but insisted
was not a "birthday
present." I have one
minute before I have
to stir the coffee so
take Tupperware out
of refrigerator and slide
into bag, then stir
coffee. Now I have
four minutes so I put
on navy blue shirt,

almost identical color
pants, put on shoes
and then go back to
bathroom for a last
look and to tie blue
and gray knit tie I got
in Italy when Alli
and I were there in
2007, the day after
we met up with Kathleen
and Art in their
apartment in Trastevere,
where Art somehow
swallowed up three
martinis in quick
succession, so was
shitfaced. He put on
a cape and led us to a
dinner of puntarelle
wet with lemon and
cured fish, gnocchi
alla romana and to
close *un piccola grappa.*
His look was tight.
And Kathleen was
one of the all-time
greats. Her look,
it has to be said,
was astonishing.
I set the one-cup
coffee maker on white
mug which says SAN
DIEGO ZOO. Fuck
the San Diego Zoo.
I wish the freedom

of all its prisoners.
But the mug is broad
and deep, carries
coffee splendidly,
I ruin it with a table-
spoon of half and
half, brisk stir with
chopstick and sit
at table. And then
I start my morning
"routine," which
starts by reading
a letter of James
Schuyler's. Today
is a letter to John
Ashbery, July 24th,
1959. Schuyler com-
plains that an
editor at *Art News*
is pressuring him to
meet a deadline and
then turns to a logistical
update about Ashbery's
possessions, which have
been left behind in an
apartment in New York,
records and books, and
I remember many years
where my person and my
things were in constant
stages of movement
between old and new
apartments, exes' places
currents places and
am glad to be in this

little house with Alli
and all my shit, although
I do have about forty
books at my office.
Schuyler closes his
letter by saying "I
will write you a long
letter from the Bingle
Barn where I will be
hard at work on my
opus THE BIG SNOOZE."
Coincidentally Alli's
alarm goes off
aspirational to wake
up this early when
there is no light in
California not even
the famous "California
light." I hear her
fingers tapping for-
ward the time,
measuring her own
not-so-big snooze.
And then I read a
poem by Emily
Dickinson. Today's goes
The Grass so little has to do –
A Sphere of simple Green –
With only Butterflies to brood
And Bees to entertain –
And stir all day to pretty Tunes
The Breezes fetch along –
And hold the Sunshine in its lap
And bow to everything –
And thread the Dews, all night, like Pearls –

And make itself so fine
A Duchess were too common
For such a noticing –
And even when it dies – to pass
In Odors so divine –
Like Lowly spices, lain to sleep –
Or Spikenards, perishing –
And then, in Sovereign Barns to dwell –
And dream the Days away,
The Grass so little has to do
I wish I were a Hay –
And I write the last
lines down in my
notebook because they
rule. And then I read
two pages of *Italian
Journey* by Goethe,
tr. W.H. Auden, a
book I bought because
John loves it and then
it sat on our shelf for
two years and I finally
realized I would
never read it all
the way through
so made it part
of my morning
routine. Today
Goethe walks around
Venice and feels
disgusted by the filth
and human feces on
the streets and claims
to have walked around
conceiving of new

civic administration of
rubbish and sewage
for the city. Then he
hurries off to the Carita
to see a monastery by
Palladio "in which he
had intended to
reproduce a typical
private home of a rich
and hospitable man
in classical times." Even
though the monastery
was only one tenth
completed Goethe thinks
it is the most sublime
structure he has ever
seen in his life. He
writes "one ought to
spend years contemplating
such a work." Sounds
nice to have so much
time for contemplating
Goethe, you asshole.
And then I read four
lines of *Oedipus Tyrannos*
by Sophocles in Greek.
Oedipus has just
been informed by
a messenger that
the guy he supposed
to be his father had
died, so no worries
Oedipus, your dad
is dead, and that old
curse that said you'd

kill your father is moot
but Oedipus is still
afraid of the prophecy's
other half, that he'd
somehow find himself
fucking his mom, right?
Which fear prompts
the messenger to soothe
his fear since the Theban
family he always thought
was his actually wasn't.
Wait, *what?*
Oedipus orders a shepherd
to come and stand for
questioning about his
birth and the four lines
I read are part of his
interrogation. Oedipus
insists you there, old
man, look me in the eyes
and answer what I ask.
Did you belong to Laios?
The shepherd says yes,
I was a slave, not bought,
but brought up in the
palace. "What work
did you do, or what
way of life did you
have?" Oedipus asks.
"For most of my life,"
the slave responds,
"I have been with the
herds." The word
Oedipus uses for
"work" is *ergon,* which

means work I guess,
but in Homer signifies
a martial act in battle
and just as often means
a "deed" or something
accomplished, like and
not like the work that
David Graeber writes
about in *Bullshit Jobs.*
Graeber might think
the shepherd derived
real satisfaction from his
enforced labor, taking joy
in the fattening sheep
destined for somebody's
dinner table, the crisp
air of outdoor Greece.
On the other hand, the
slave would never savor
the delicious rind of
braised lamb melted
into feral butter. He
wouldn't even see the
table unless he was
setting it. Like a lot
of us I guess who go
to work. The ancient form
of *ergon* had another
letter in front of it, a
letter which ended
up disappearing from
Attic Greek which is
called the digamma.
It was a voiced labio-
velar approximant,

which is represented
by the English letter
"w" in English so *ergon*
was originally pronounced
wergon and is cognate
with the English word
"work." Sophocles con-
cludes my "routine" so
I put books in neat stack
for tomorrow morning
put mug in the sink and
rinse, then put on blue
jacket Alli found, a jacket
I count one of the world's
great treasures. What
Bob called my "French
worker jacket" and what
Alli said was a "Bill
Cunningham jacket"
they are both right, put
backpack on, lock door
behind me, walk into
bracing black morning.
I walk up San Diego
street and cross and I
see this guy who I see
almost every morning
walking down San Diego
street presumably on his
way to work. We always
both have headphones
on and somehow we got
into the habit of saying
good morning to each
other and looking each

other in the eyes although
we have never spoken
or met in any way.
And then I listen to
Britney Spears. I don't
know why I woke up
with "Hold It Against
Me" in my head but I'm
grateful to the gods of
pop for intervening in
my sleep and I always
try to obey their commands.
I listen to it perilously
loud, Britney's voice
polishes morning. It might
as well be the only
song in the universe.
It's so engrossing
I forget to notice
the short blocks
between Belmont
Avenue and San Pablo
Avenue. When it
concludes, I let my
phone decide what
other songs by Britney
Spears will soundtrack
my walk. The sinuous
strings of "Toxic"
sustain me as I cross
San Pablo and cut
through the parking lot
of the Pic n'Pac where
two cars are parked,
their drivers waiting

impatiently for big cold
first drink of beer.
And then a song called
"Work Bitch" arrives
on my device. "Work
Bitch" is a nadir of Britney,
an act of exhaustive
and incoherent appropriation.
Britney clearly steals the
tempo and motifs of
"Work Bitch" from
Black drag culture in
New York, essentially
cosplaying as Madonna
on her worst behavior.
Like she uses a Cockney
accent. Whatever is not
Alabama I guess, poor
Britney, poor baby
leave Britney alone.
But Britney, and Madonna
certainly, is of course
exactly the kind of
USAmerican who would
go to London for a week
vacation and come
back "smoking fags"
devastating slang,
inappropriately
offering "Bob's
Your Uncle" when the
situation calls for a simple
"how daft." Mean-
while "Work Bitch"
pivots from the

celebration of simple
fabulousness to a catalogue
of material delights which
can be obtained, according
to Spears, by hard work.
"You better make it to
work, bitch." I don't make it
to the end of "Work Bitch,"
sorry Britney. I cross Kearney
and Liberty and then cut
through the parking lot
of the BART station, check
the screen and see the Millbrae
train is in one minute so
quicken pace, jog upstairs
to the platform, panting as
the train pours in. Punk Rock
Jeff is in my train car,
no surprise. I met Punk
Rock Jeff in 1998.
Jodi introduced us at
the café in Cole Valley
where I worked and by
coincidence Punk Rock Jeff
had reviewed my zine
in *Maximum Rock n'Roll*.
I ran into him a few times
for a while and always
admired his astonishingly
bad mood. Punk Rock Jeff's
face always looks like
someone farted next to him
and still does. I see him
almost every morning.
I never talk to him, but

always wonder if he
remembers me. The train
is packed so I give up on
the book, stick with
headphones. I listen to
Sir Babygirl sing "Flirting
With Her," a song I
especially love to listen
to in the morning
and particularly the part
where Sir Babygirl sings
she left her name on my lips
I don't think I'll ever get over her hips
Or ever feel like anything else exists
When she texts me 'hey!'
it reminds me of the
famous basic obsessiveness,
verging on nihilism,
of starting to fall in love
with someone. A guy
with a guitar brushes
past, pausing in front
of me to tell the assembled
captive group he is
raising money for his
kids' physical therapy.
I have paid him
before but can't even
listen to him play now.
He only plays one
song, every day,
over and over,
"Imagine" by John
Lennon, and while
there are often whole

eras of my life defined
by listening to one song
over and over again,
I think "Imagine" is
only so so and the guy is,
I'm sorry, not that good.
Neither he or "Imagine"
can conceivably compete
with the solar reach of
"Flirting With Her."
The train bewails
into downtown Berkeley.
I ride the escalator to the
top, careful not to touch
the rubber moving rails,
because I read an article
about the sheer volume
of piss and shit that coats
the BART escalators which
is the primary reason,
according to BART,
that they are always out
of service. I emerge onto
the still-gray plaza and
cross Center street. A guy
lumbers past me
pushing a bicycle
yelling out loud I NEED
SOMEONE TO FUCKING
FIX THIS over and over
as he walks down Shattuck
towards the Berkeley
Public Library. I walk
past the Wells Fargo
ATMs which were wonder-

fully destroyed during
the riot that met Milo
Yannipoulis when he came
to Berkeley to try and speak
to a gathered group of white
supremacists, neo-nazis,
fascists, emissaries from
the ugly pond peoples
of furthest Kekistan,
and unaffiliated right
wing fuckfaces. Then
the great stores of
Shattuck Avenue: Seasons
of Japan, the Berkeley
Hearing Center, Sushi
Secrets, Happy Lemon,
Flying Falafel, places
I have never been to.
I cross Addison in front
of the Half Price Books
and take a left, pausing
 to look at the first panel
of the Berkeley Poetry Walk
See! I am dancing!
On the rim of the world I am dancing!
The plaque notes this text is
an Ohlone song. The walk
continues down Addison.
Jack London, George Sterling,
Robinson Jeffers. Witter
Bynner, Li Po, Hildegarde
Flanner, Genevieve Taggard.
An excerpt of Robert Duncan's
"The Structure of Rime II,"
a poem and poet I have

never really figured out.
But I remember looking at
this plaque. Aaron gave
a reading after which he told
me that for a while he and
Duncan were lovers and
that Duncan had written
a love poem for him
and I who love gossip
asked Aaron what the
title of the poem is and I
found the poem and it was
so beautiful, and it wasn't
like a regular Robert
Duncan poem with a bunch
of talking lions and other
esoteric wisdom from
etheric Messengers or
whatever. Just kidding.
When Duncan describes
the moment their bodies
come together to fuck
he describes it as becoming
"one trunk" and I loved
that so much. Then Jack
Spicer and Robin Blaser,
and I am full of nostalgia
for moving to the Bay Area
when I was young and
learning about these poets
from people who had known
them or still know them,
and particularly Kevin
Killian, whose birthday is
in two days, Christmas

Eve. Then a couple
plaques obscured by
expectant trash cans.
In front of the theater
they have cunningly placed
poems by William Shakespeare,
Ben Jonson, Thornton
Wilder, Bertold Brecht,
Ntozake Shange, and Tony
Kushner. Then Lyn
Hejinian's poem—hi Lyn!
Then some more panels
of poets I don't know and
then a bunch I do know
or did know, like Leslie
Scalapino, Brenda Hillman,
Ron Silliman, Jean Day,
Laura Moriarty, Carla
Harryman, Bob Perelman,
and I consider crossing
the street to go look at
the panel with some lyrics
from OPERATION IVY'S
"Knowledge" which always
gives me great pleasure,
but I am not going to cross
the street and delay my walk
so instead I put on "Knowledge"
and it buoys me, as it has
since I first played it on
a little boombox in my
parent's bathroom when
I was 15. *All I know*
is that I don't know.
All I know is that I don't

know nothing!
I cross Milvia and turn
right in front of the ACE
Hardware and walk up
the street past the ugly
new condos and wait for
the light to turn at
University Avenue, which
it does and I walk across
the street and turn left
until I reach the doors of
1995 University Avenue
at 7:44 a.m. and push doors
and walk past H&R
Block sign that reads
OWN YOUR TOMORROW
and say good morning
to the morning security
guard, about whom I know
little except that she smokes
cigarettes and has the most
amazing way of saying
the word "Okay." She
says good morning
and I push the up
button on the elevator
and hear a little ding
and the doors open
and I walk into it.

Brandon Brown is the author of several books, most recently *The Four Seasons* (Wonder) and *The Good Life* (Big Lucks.) He has edited the zines *Fuck You Longhair, Dee Dee's Kids, Sleep is the Enemy, Commonweal, OMG!, Celebrity Brush* and currently edits *Panda's Friend*. He lives in the shadows of Albany Hill in El Cerrito, California.

WORK was printed in an edition of
750 copies at McNaughton & Gunn, Inc.
Text and cover design and typesetting by Derek Fenner
using the old-style serif typeface Garamond.

Atelos was founded in 1995 as a project of Hips Road and is devoted to publishing, under the sign of poetry, writing that challenges conventional, limiting definitions of poetry. All the works published as part of the Atelos project are commissioned specifically for it, and each is involved in some way with crossing traditional genre boundaries, including, for example, those that would separate theory from practice, poetry from prose, essay from drama, the visual image from the verbal, the literary from the non-literary, and so forth. The Atelos project when complete will consist of 50 volumes.

The project directors and editors are Lyn Hejinian and Travis Ortiz. The director for design, cover production, and text production is Derek Fenner.

Distributed by:

Small Press Distribution
1341 Seventh Street
Berkeley, California
94710-1403

Atelos
P O Box 5814
Berkeley, California
94705-0814

to order from SPD call 510-524-1668 or toll-free 800-869-7553

fax orders to: 510-524-0852

order via e-mail at: orders@spdbooks.org

order online from: www.spdbooks.org